THE TYRANNY
OF ALGORITHMS

Miguel Benasayag

THE TYRANNY
OF ALGORITHMS

A CONVERSATION
WITH RÉGIS MEYRAN

*Translated from the French
by Steven Rendall*

Europa
editions

Europa Editions
1 Penn Plaza, Suite 6282
New York, N.Y. 10019
www.europaeditions.com
info@europaeditions.com

Copyright © Édition Textuel, 2019
13 Quai de Conti - 75006 Paris
www.editionstextuel.com
First Publication 2021 by Europa Editions

Translation by Steven Rendall
Original title: *La Tyrannie des algorithmes*
Translation copyright © 2021 by Europa Editions

Library of Congress Cataloging in Publication Data is available
ISBN 978-1-60945-662-7

Benasayag, Miguel
The Tyranny of Algorithms

Book design by Emanuele Ragnisco
instagram.com/emanueleragnisco

Cover image by Ginevra Rapisardi

Prepress by Grafica Punto Print – Rome

Printed and bound in Great Britain by Clays Ltd, Elcograf S.p.A.

CONTENTS

THE TYRANNY
OF ALGORITHMS

Preface

We read all sorts of things about AI. In general, it is presented either as the promise of a future happiness—indeed, as the possibility of becoming superhuman and attaining immortality, according to the credo of the promoters of transhumanism, from Yuval Harari to Laurent Alexandre—or as a threat capable of putting an end to humanity, as in science fiction films like *Terminator*, among advocates of a complete return to nature, and in survivalist groups. But more serious and less fanciful reflection leads us to see that we cannot be "for" or "against" AI, insofar as it is already here and is not likely to disappear any time soon. The question we now face is rather how to exist *qua* human beings, individually, socially, collectively, in a world governed in large measure by algorithms. That is the question that Miguel Benasayag seeks to explore in these conversations. A philosopher and psychoanalyst of Argentine origin, a former resistance fighter active in the wake of Che Guevara, Benasayag here builds upon his earlier reflections on the relationship between living beings and machines.[1]

[1] See *Cerveau augmenté, homme diminué* (La Découverte, 2016), *La Singularité du vivant* (Le Pommier, 2017), and, most recently, *Fonctionner ou exister* (Le Pommier, 2018).

One of his most decisive contributions to the current debate is his demonstration of the specificity of the phenomenon of life: the human being is not analogous to a machine, contrary to an idea widespread in the public at large, as well as among scientists (in fields ranging from the neurosciences to biology).

The analogy between living beings and machines completely obscures the former's peculiarities: not only does the living being include a share of "negativity" (it is always burdened by various malfunctions and poor adaptations to the environment); it also operates in accord with a logic that Benasayag describes as *integrative*. That is, an organism is not a simple collection of organs, each of which executes specific functions, any more than it is reducible to a given amount of information—that might be duplicated independently of its medium. Nevertheless, the work of computer scientists and AI specialists is shaped by these epistemological errors: for them, the brain is nothing more than a computer. As we will see, the consequences are disastrous for our freedoms.

This brings us to the second point in Benasayag's thought that must be emphasized to make it easy to follow these conversations, namely the distinction he makes between *functioning* and *existing*. Since the dawn of humanity, technological objects have been hybridized with the human mind: it is we who have shaped them, but as we use them, they in turn shape our brain. With the development of new technologies (the internet, Big Data, the new generation of algorithms, social networks, applications for smartphones, etc.), this hybridization is becoming more and more apparent, and machines now threaten to colonize us if we use them badly.

Constant and immediate interactions via Facebook and Twitter, immersion in virtual reality through video games, engaging in athletics while connected to devices that measure and record our performance, the use of GPS in our cars . . . these all involve programs that interfere in our lives without our having always chosen to use them. For Benasayag, if we are not capable of controlling our use of these programs, we are reduced to no longer existing, but only functioning, like machines—that is, reduced to pure efficiency and performance. An advertisement in the subway for music online, describing individuals as being "in pause mode" when they relax or "in repetition mode" when they are running on a treadmill, is a good metaphor for such a danger. Are we doomed, from now on, to be just performers of a set of routines whose omnipresence weakens our moments of consciousness (including boredom, error, doubt . . .) and our capacities of imagination and concentration—in short, our ability to exist?

But, taking as our point of departure this need to resist colonization by machines on the personal level, in these conversations we also ask what impact the digital world and algorithms have on our societies. Yes, AI allows us to make many kinds of work easier (for example, by helping physicians with certain diagnoses), but these benefits often come at the cost of reducing people to sets of micro-data (the websites we visit, our purchases, etc., make it possible to "predict," for instance, deviant behavior) and digital profiles, far removed from the human beings and their element of unforeseeability and freedom. Worse yet: the whole economy, that of large companies, financial markets, and states, is now subject to the "decisions" suggested by machines. We have entered, Benasayag tells us, the era of algorithmic governmentality in which leaders have knowingly delegated their decision-making to AI: a factory, a hospital, or a railroad has to be closed because algorithmic analysis has determined that it is unprofitable.

How, then, can we still talk about democracy? And, consequently, how can we organize collective action when confronted by a power based on the supposed infallibility of machines? Rejecting the great emancipatory narratives of the last century, Benasayag thinks that only small resistance groups, deciding to act here and now, will be able to thwart the tyranny of algorithms: in discussion groups, periodicals, and publishing houses seeking to foil ideologies; in associations aiding migrants and homeless people; in resistance zones (ZADs) where the inhabitants see themselves not as defending nature but rather as being part of it. That is, in groups that occupy terrain with their bodies, that de-virtualize social and individual life, and that are capable of increasingly colonizing digital machines in the service of emancipation. Let us hope that these conversations will help bring about a return of these conflict zones, which are necessary guarantees of democracy and freedom.

Régis Meyran

THE FAILURE OF WESTERN RATIONALITY

To begin by setting the scene, explain your criticism of the expression "artificial intelligence" (AI).

In reality, what we call "artificial intelligence" is very badly named. In this expression, the word "intelligence" is only a metaphor. Even if its calculative ability exceeds that of human beings, artificial intelligence is incapable of giving a meaning to its own calculations. It is essential to distinguish the machine's functioning from the intelligence of living beings, because living intelligence is not a calculating machine. It is a process that articulates affectivity, corporeality, and error and that presupposes the presence of desire and a consciousness, in human beings, of one's own long-term history. Human intelligence is not conceivable independently of all our other cerebral and bodily processes. To be intelligent, you have to have a body: the body is the site of passions, drives, long-term memory; it is where the memory of my parents or grandparents is reincarnated, where even the memory of the species' evolution is conveyed!

Which is not the case for AI . . .

Contrary to animals, which think with the help of a brain housed within a body, which is itself situated within an environment, the machine has no body. AI produces calculations and predictions independently of any meaning. The question that the media so often dwell upon—whether a machine can be substituted for a human being—is therefore absurd, because it is the living being, and not calculation, that creates meaning. Some AI researchers are convinced that the difference between living intelligence and artificial intelligence is quantitative, but it is qualitative. The dominant point of view, even among researchers, maintains that the brain's structure and processes are analogous to those of a machine with discrete states. That is why the living being is treated and formatted according to this credo, while ignoring what I call the singularity of the living. The latter has nothing to do with any kind of vitalism but instead refers to the radical difference between functioning and existing. Existence cannot dispense with functions, but neither can it be reduced and subjected to them.

However, today, humans have enormous confidence in AI, delegating more and more functions to it at both the individual and collective levels. In our cars, we get our bearings by using GPS; if on foot, we use a mobile application. Stock markets rely on AI to make decisions affecting whole countries. I would like to begin by saying why we have, at this point, so much confidence in the machine. To do that, we have to dive back into the history of Western rationality.

What does the history of Western rationality tell us about the advent of AI?

It all begins with one of the major events in human history, of which we are more or less contemporaries because it takes place around 1900 and marks the end of the historical cycle of modernity. This event takes the form of a crisis of rationality.

Modernity is "the epoch of Man," as Michel Foucault calls it. Although we know when modernity ends, it is hard to say precisely when it begins. It has its origin in the philosopher Peter Abelard, among others, around 1100, when the young nominalists began to assert that people have to think for themselves. Abelard was convicted in a trial held in Soissons: he was accused of having tried "to see without a veil." "Seeing without a veil" and "thinking for oneself" are formulas that foreshadow a new mode of thought and that have, contrary to what one think, nothing to do with current individualism. Rather, it is the idea that each of us is a singularity, a unit, that contains the universe as a whole. With this new idea, the individual is freed from the community and begins to think as a subject. But it is also an analogical mode of thought: the "whole" of the individual is analogous to the whole of the universe. Henceforth, Man, by understanding himself, can understand the universe. In addition, it is also a break with the authority of the Church and with the feudal lord. This new tradition of thought continues all the way to Johannes Kepler and Galileo. For Kepler, "the only difference between God and men is that God has always known all the theorems, whereas men do not yet know them all."

But how does the advent of rationalism change the way Westerners see the world?

Rationalism breaks with a medieval, cyclical tradition of time: now there exists a rectilinear path to be followed that leads to more knowledge and, finally, to a totality with which the human being will be the equivalent of God. The path blazed by Galileo says that the universe was written in a mathematical language. The world is organized according to a geometrical model that it is possible to understand thanks to mathematical laws—consider Isaac Newton, who describes the planets' revolutions using the laws of universal gravitation. Modernity's project is thus to free itself from both authority and the group to describe a world organized by reason. Therefore, the instrument of this emancipation of Western humanity is reason; it is even the promise of total reason.

In this history, of course we must mention René Descartes and his project for Man, who is to become the "master and possessor" of nature, but above all, we must mention Immanuel Kant, who thought that in his time humanity was ready to attain its "maturity": henceforth, it would be governed by reason alone. We can also mention Georg Wilhelm Friedrich Hegel, for whom humanity guides itself toward the age of the spirit: for him, history is a long progress of discoveries and accomplishments culminating in an epoch in which human rationality will be able to govern the whole universe.

Isn't this project of mastering history and the universe by reason also to be found in the nineteenth century, in Charles Darwin and Karl Marx?

Darwin's scientific discoveries were broadly interpreted by Teilhard de Chardin and Francis Galton, but Darwin did not present his discoveries as a linear ascent that would lead to total discovery. Darwin was more complex than the trend he gave birth to: he didn't even put humankind at the apex of the pyramid of living beings. On the other hand, Marx was completely caught up in a linear view of history as a necessary and teleological progress that would lead to total knowledge. In his work, we find again the idea of a science to be formulated, of a rationality to be found.

However, in *The Descent of Man*,[2] Darwin sketches out the idea of a process of civilization that is gradually established and would allow the emergence of moral consciousness and reason.

Yes, but for him moral consciousness is a behavior acquired in the course of evolution that is very important for life in society and is the result of natural selection; it is not an accomplishment. However that may be, rational thought was to engender a whole set of practices, some good, others bad. But the great novelty is the idea that there is only one single world.

[2] Charles Darwin, *The Descent of Man* (1871).

Didn't humanistic thought already maintain that there is only one world?

Up to this point, despite the advent of modernity, there existed not one world but a plurality of worlds, nesting one within the other. Modernity and humanism invented the idea of a common humanity, a common base for all humans. The expression of this emergent humanism might be illustrated, for example, by the Valladolid controversy (1550–1551), which set the Dominican monk Bartolomé de las Casas against the theologian Juan Ginés de Sepulveda. This polemic bore on the question of whether the Amerindians were humans and, thus, whether they had souls. Nonetheless, it is interesting to note that Las Casas, though siding with the Amerindians, says that they are humans "with unaccomplished [i.e., incomplete] humanity." Although he won this argument against the Vatican, it was a somewhat Pyrrhic victory: by considering the Amerindians as humans on the path to full development, humanism would later make it possible to justify colonialism, since now the West was going to assign itself the mission of "accomplishing," whatever the cost, the humanity of non-Western peoples, as well as that of women. It is thus the idea that the white, rational man would be the leader, placing himself at the top of the scale of progress with all the others below him because they are not yet complete humans. Similarly, children have an unaccomplished humanity, which will justify mistreating them during their upbringing . . . The same structure will justify beating people who are ill, mad, or deviant, to accomplish their humanity.

But is there a necessary causal relationship between rationality and the structure of domination?

The worldview I've just described depends on the existence of theories and practices founded on the idea that rationality allows us to determine possible futures. Rationality makes it possible to control the past, the present, and the future. In this way, it connects the spaces of freedom and domination. I am free thanks to rationality, because I can free myself from the real by freeing myself from its constraints. Modernity thus comes to associate freedom with domination: the free man will be the one who dominates others and dominates himself.

Consequently, the enterprise of rationalizing the world leads to the importance given to technology and medicine, but also to colonialism, slavery, massacres, and the transformation of everything into merchandise. The other characteristic of rationalism is that it eliminates all elements of reality that cannot be modeled quantitatively.

So in modernity, the ambition was to strive for a complete modeling of the world?

We can cite Husserl when he refers to Galileo's project of using mathematics to found a "realm of truly objective knowledge" and his hypothesis according to which "there must be methods of measurement for everything that geometry, the mathematics of forms, includes in its ideality and its *a priori* nature." According to this hypothesis, even "specifically qualitative processes must be indirectly co-mathematized." Although there is in fact a claim to an all-encompassing modeling of reality and of nature, the latter nonetheless remains in the complex domain of mathematics, which exists, as the mathematician Giuseppe Longo explains,[3] at "the interface between us and the real, which generates friction, of course, and channels the cognitive act, but which is organized by the same act." In this interface of the production of mathematical knowledge, we are thus once again confronted by a function of the real in the mode of "not everything is possible." In other words, the mathematization of the world as Galileo imagined it represents a horizon that, even though it organizes the possible practices, remains out of reach. Like social utopias, five-year plans, and various ideologies that seek to control the field of the living, this type of referential model functions by constantly confronting the real with bodies that it tries to discipline, thus producing and reproducing a profound conflictuality.

How does the Galilean project of mathematicizing nature differ from the vast digitalization we are witnessing today?

Mathematical language, like the world of language in general and that of writing, actually seeks to make the territory resemble the map. However, it does not deny the

[3] Francis Bailly and Giuseppe Longo, "Causalités et symétries dans les sciences de la nature. Le continu et le discret mathématiques," in Jean-Baptiste Joinet (ed.), *Logique, dynamique et cognition*. Paris: Presses de la Sorbonne, 2007.

otherness of the territory, which continues to exist in a conflictual relationship with the map. And this dynamic determines the lines of non-compossibility that limit and modify the map in return. Conversely, in the digital world, the principle "everything is information" considers territories as a simple mode of the map's existence. The violence of digitalization thus resides not in some project of domination, but rather in the negation of all forms of alterity and singular identity to make room for a dimension of pure abstraction. Anything in the territory (the reality of bodies, of ecosystems . . .) that resists attempts at modeling thus becomes, in the world of digital models, "noise in the system."

The illusion of an algorithmic reality thus ignores what Alan Turing already warned us against when he asserted that even in arithmetic, not everything is calculable. A characteristic specific to every complex set is precisely the impossibility of representing all its elements—that is, the non-representability and incomplete calculability of the slightest biological organism. Thus, the problem resides not in AI or the digital model, but in the interpretation of their power, which seeks to absorb the territory into the map.

But haven't there always been, from the sixteenth century on, thinkers who have sought to resist that rationalist temptation, or at least to conceive rationality in a less caricatural way? I'm thinking about the works of folklorists in France, who, from Paul Sébillot to Arnold van Gennep, have documented and analyzed

popular knowledge, taking its richness into account and not dismissing it as "noise in the system."

Even thinkers like Gottfried Wilhelm Leibniz and Baruch Spinoza, who fall entirely within the field of rationality, did not adhere to the project of a knowable and calculable whole. It's enough to consider, for example, the importance Spinoza accords in his *Ethics* (which he presents *"more geometrico"*) to the non-knowledge of what a body can do at the heart of the system. Similarly, Leibniz, in his completely deterministic system, rejects the fatalism of complete predictability. Thus, he indicates clearly the limits of predictable reasoning, notably distinguishing between what is analytically possible and what is really "compossible," in other words, that with which reality comes to terms . . . For him, what can be conceived rationally is the whole of the "theoretically possible," in which there exists a subset that contains what can really exist. Thus, the Other of the rationally possible is not the irrational, but the existent and its complexity.

Moreover, we have to recognize that for thinkers who adhere to the dialectical method, negativity is organically incorporated. Thus, for Hegel, even as he maintains the idea of a totalizing totality, the dialectical path toward that utopia of pure positivity requires the work of the negative. In the same way, for Marx, the endpoint of the historical path that he presents as scientific Communism requires contradiction. For him, the negative will be presented in the form of scarcity, injustice, or poverty, that is, in signs that he interprets as symptoms of the blocked development of productive forces by the maintenance of old relations of production. By the way, let us add that the non-realizable character of the final utopia ("the age of the spirit" or "scientific Communism") does not, obviously, invalidate the still fundamental interest of their works.

It is here that we find the break incarnated by the digital world—or, at least, the technocratic aspirations of the use of digital technologies. Some claim that the digital world embodies a complete positivity that is already possible. But from my phenomenological point of view, "negativity" is the central axis and even the condition of existence: it is evoked by what, today, we identify as the irrational, the instinctual, the sacrificial, the sacred, and even bodies themselves in their complexity . . . At another level, it's also manifested by the non-adaptability and the "unfitting" side of the living being.

Let's move forward in time a bit. If I understand correctly, rationalism suffers an initial defeat at the beginning of the twentieth century. But aren't there, later on, hyperrationalist trends, such as eugenics, whose defenders seek to fabricate a pure and ideal society, rid of allegedly deficient and unproductive elements?

To be clear: we call the belief that makes an unreasonable use of reason "rationalism." Now, what we call the crisis of epistemological foundations that occurs around 1900 does not affect solely rationalist belief, far from it. It involves a genuine transformation of the myths and contents of the whole of rationality. Contrary to what metaphysical rationalism claims, rationality still retains a conflictual and consonant relationship with historical development. Thus the universal character of the principles of rationality must not be virtualized to the point of becoming abstract. The problems that rationality takes up and that transform it are still epochal. We have to see rationality as a requirement rather than as a collection of definitive elements. In that sense, rationality can't be separated from any question of meaning. Its principles are constructed in response to concrete problems that include non-arbitrary relations of contiguity and continuity, and they therefore correspond in large measure to what Spinoza calls the second kind of knowledge, or knowledge by causes. Rational knowledge is always a knowledge of relationships.

Conversely, digital hyperrationalism is founded on purely quantitative correlations based on the dislocation of any set, and today it may still represent, more than some fundamentalisms, a major manifestation of the irrational. Whence our contemporaries' entirely legitimate complaint when confronted by the brutal application of macroeconomic models: they point out that "all this is not logical" and don't know how right they ultimately are.

You think the crisis of rationality coincides with taking complexity into account in our relationship to knowledge. Can you explain that?

Let's return to the break that occurs around 1900: from that moment on, we can no longer affirm that rationality is limited to what is analytically foreseeable.

To put it another way, it is a moment of encounter with complexity, to use Edgar Morin's concept.[4] For him, complexity is not a discovery or a construction, but an encounter. In mathematical science, in 1900, we witness a "foundational crisis," as David Hilbert called it. Then an effort is made to salvage a complete and consistent axiomatics, but without succeeding in expelling any principle of contradiction from the heart of the combinatorics. Analogous processes were first produced in the hard sciences with quantum and relativity physics, but also in the human sciences with the Freudian theory of the unconscious and the "id." In art, this movement of deconstruction affected the esthetic archetypes that had been dominant up to that time. This was also the case in history, with the emergence of the "Annales School," which questioned the delimitation of historical facts.

But of course, as you emphasize, rationalism was going to persist despite everything, even though it no longer had a rational foundation! After the period from 1900 to 1920, any attempt at a theory that would eliminate the unpredictable dimension of events was no longer rational. In the mathematical and physical sciences, elements emerging from the break were taken into account and incorporated organically. To a lesser extent, this was also the case for the human sciences and art. On the other hand, in the political and social world, such a

[4] Edgar Morin, *Introduction à la pensée complexe*. Paris: ESF, 1990.

break and its challenges were radically unknown. In the political field, people continued to march and to sacrifice themselves behind leaders and programs that continued to assume that rationality could be identified with the linearity of the predictable, the utilitarian, and the countable.

So, after 1920, rationalism was a kind of survival of an old way of thinking that's outmoded today?

Exactly. We have to see rationality as a historically constructed system with a variable geometry. Some elements are situated at the heart of such a system and all of a sudden find themselves rejected, relegated to the edge of the irrational, or even completely eliminated. Physicians long considered the use of leeches attached to patients' bodies rational, before that practice became irrational. Other elements lost their universal character and became more local rationalities. For example, Newton's theory of gravity was regionalized and cohabited with Albert Einstein's general theory of relativity. Conversely, other elements that were earlier considered completely irrational entered the field of rationality—as did, notably, the aleatory. Thus it is now appropriate to integrate the unpredictable into rational thought about the limits of reason.

What are the theories that bring the irrational into rationality? I am thinking about the theory of catastrophes elaborated by the mathematician René Thom, starting in 1968.

Of course, Thom proposes a theory that seeks to think rationally about the limits of rationality. But there are also the two theorems of incompleteness that Kurt Gödel established in the 1930s—the second theorem notably implying that a coherent demonstration does not demonstrate its own coherence. There is also Paul Cohen's critique of constructible sets in the 1960s. In physics, there is the irruption of the quantum theory of physics and relativity physics in the work of Max Planck in 1900, then in that of Niels Bohr, Albert Einstein, Werner Heisenberg, and more. Already in 1900, many articles commented on this event and asked whether quantum theory did not abolish the real. If everything is made of atoms and atoms are made of particles but the particles are not really there—because we only identify a density of the probability of their presence—then what is reality?

What is the consequence of this explosion of rationalist convictions?

The great break in 1900 produced a shock effect: all at once, the edifice based on the idea that white, Western, rational males had to dominate the subject suddenly collapsed. As a result, we witness a return of religiousness and, furthermore, a rise of relativism in all its forms, particularly cultural. Western humanity is disoriented by its uneasiness about the nature of the real, by another way of writing history that would include the study of "the housewife's shopping bag" instead of kings and battles, as the *Annales* historians put it. Thus, we witness a breaking-up of the object of study. At that point, we see emerging in the 1930s a very strong mysticism—a marked interest in Buddhism, Islam . . . But the most important event is that Western thought, instead of pausing and challenging itself, kept going and became the victim, in my opinion in a completely unpredictable way, of an "unfortunate encounter" with the digital world.

The 1930s also saw the invention of Western esotericism with authors like René Guénon, who proposed a new, artificial synthesis of various traditional ideas and had a profound impact on the intellectuals of his time.[5]

In the nineteenth century, spiritualism was already very fashionable among intellectuals. Look at the American essayist Ralph Waldo Emerson: he tried to contact spirits using electricity. But actually, the two world wars accentuated this movement away from rationalism. And between the two wars, the end of overweening Western pride was made complete. Nonetheless, the "unfortunate encounter" with computer science took place immediately after the Second World War. In my view, the importance acquired by computer science then resulted from the fact that humanity was somewhat disoriented because its central axis, reason victorious, was failing. What was at that time

[5] Pierre Lagrange and Claudie Voisenat, *L'Ésoterisme contemporain et ses lecteurs. Entre savoirs, croyances et fictions.* Paris: BPI/Centre Pompidou, 2005, foreword by Daniel Fabre.

called "cybernetics" renewed the promise of a total, complete rationality, consistent and conquering—but at a very high price: that of delegating decisions and control from the human to the machine.

So it's the failure of rationality that leads to artificial intelligence?

It's not rationality in itself that has failed: it's rationalism, that is, an exaggerated and unreasonable belief in reason. Rationality, as a constructed historical whole, with a variable geometry, is not disappearing; instead, it's undergoing a very important transformation. From this point on, it does not declare previous knowledge abolished, it declares it insufficient. For example, Einstein's theory of general relativity does not abolish Newton's theory. In certain frameworks, it is simply better to think in Newtonian terms, and in others it is better to think in Einsteinian terms. If I jump off a sixth-floor balcony because I think Newton was wrong, I am making a terrible mistake; in this framework, you have to think in Newtonian terms! What is no longer appropriate is to call this the theory of "universal gravitation" because it is no longer universal and absolute—but it remains universal on the surface of a planet. So it's not the possibility of an objective knowledge that is disappearing: it's a quasi-religious belief.

So rationalism can be seen as myth of reason as our savior?

Yes, it is a myth, which is going to be reborn from its ashes as it invades the domain of computer science.

But why is rationalism reborn from its ashes at the end of the Second World War in the form of computer science?

It seems to me that there's a group of factors that explains this grand return of rationalism. Major events like the Holocaust, Hiroshima, and Nagasaki have changed the situation. Take the example of the Armenian genocide of 1915: no one thought this event challenged Western rationality. My grandfather had to flee Turkey because he helped Armenians at the time of the genocide. He told us that this event was an absolute horror, but no one at the time asked, "Can we write poetry after the Armenian genocide? Can we go on thinking after the Armenian genocide?" World opinion considers the Armenian genocide a major fact, but not an event that creates a break between a "before" and an "after."

On the other hand, with the Holocaust, a fissure appeared in rationality. And all the more so because it emanated from Germany, the messianic land of rationality, one might say. Marx, for example, thought that Germany and England were the two countries of the avant-garde where socialism might arise. Germany was the country of the great thinkers of rationality, from Immanuel Kant to Martin Heidegger. But Heidegger adhered to national socialism . . . These German brains finally showed, at the end of the Second World War, that it is possible to think about evil rationally, whereas before we were convinced that thinking rationally led us to think of good.

Can you explain a little more: what does an event like the Shoah change in our relation to rationality?

In 1900, the first break in rationality only concerned scientists and artists. With Auschwitz, it began to concern everyone. Up to this point, the hypothesis of modernity, found in Descartes and Kant, could be formulated this way: "He who thinks well, thinks of the good." That meant that someone who uses reason's instruments well can only arrive at the good. There is a hypothesis of consubstantiality between using reason well and doing good—just as science could not fail to develop for the good of humanity. But with Auschwitz and Hiroshima, we realize that people who thought very well were led to think well about evil. The other consequence, which is much less tragic, is that people who don't think "rationally" from the point of view of mathematical logic can nonetheless think about the good. All individuals, no matter how uneducated or uncultured, and any people, no matter what their technological development, can, in spite of everything, emancipate themselves and direct themselves toward the good. This is the beginning of Third-World thought.

Auschwitz is in fact the consequence of a rational and scientific plan for the mass extermination of several minorities—Jews, Gypsies, homosexuals.

Yes, it was a scientific calculation and an implementation of technology. But behind that is reason at work, as was advocated by Heidegger, the great philosopher who never renounced his adherence to Nazism.

We have recently seen, notably with the publication of Heidegger's "Black Notebooks," the importance of anti-semitism in his thought, including his philosophical thought.[6]

That's true, but, really, Heidegger has been criticized regularly and cyclically since 1945. Whereas, moreover, he continued to be adored in France and was notably quoted by Jacques Lacan, Alain Badiou, and others. Now, as psychoanalysis points out, the whole problem is that someone who reasons extremely well can end up taking pleasure in evil. Rationality is therefore not a barrier to this. It sometimes happens that a people gives itself over to this kind of pleasure—as is the case today in Italy, with Matteo Salvini in power, in Brazil with Jair Bolsonaro, in France with Marine Le Pen . . . So we see that there are moments in history when the masses reject any form of complex thought and become addicted to brutish pleasure. This pleasure in populism goes perfectly with the advent of a post-democratic digital world.

[6] See Andrew J. Mitchell and Peter Trawny, *Heidegger's Black Notebooks: Responses to Anti-Semitism.* New York: Columbia University Press, 2017.

"This pleasure in populism goes perfectly with the advent of a post-democratic digital world."

But how is this related to AI?

How is it related? Well, a major event occurred: after the West's fit of narcissism that we call the Second World War, intellectuals were excited about cybernetics, a discipline that would seek to establish analogies between living organisms and machines. This science adopts the rationalist promise, that of a humanity guided by reason, which seemed to have completely failed. Cybernetics opens the way to a new stage in the delegation of functions from the human to technology. The myth of Icarus showed humans that they cannot fly, so instead technology allows them to construct an airplane. The cybernetic promise is based in part on the idea of technology as liberation from work and the difficulty of life, as was already the case in the works of Marx or Comte. But the latter were thinking of the machine in the service of humans.

But isn't there a big difference between the emancipatory promise of technology and artificial intelligence? Isn't the idea of a machine that is (supposedly) able to think for itself new?

At the outset, that idea is found in science fiction writers. Mary Shelley's *Frankenstein, or the Modern Prometheus* (1818) takes up an old theme, the Jewish myth of the Golem. But the digital world goes further, claiming that the machine can say "I" and make decisions because it is created, we are told, by reproducing the material elements constitutive of the living being and of the brain, and allegedly improving them through augmentation. The digital's view of the world "as a Lego set" has spread to today's neurosciences and artificial intelligence. We need only remember the task assigned us by the neurobiologist Jean-Pierre Changeux. In *L'Homme neuronal*,[7] published in 1983, he claims that "the barrier between the mental and the neural can be abolished." The mental is thought, feelings . . . Changeux reduces all that to the purely neural: for him, it's nothing but cerebral wiring. And this cerebral wiring is in fact a digital conception of the mind.

Wasn't cybernetics based, from the beginning, on a reductionism (thought is reduced to electrical currents in the brain) and an analogy (the brain is analogous to a computer)?

In the first theory of information proposed by the American engineer and mathematician Claude Shannon, there was still no question of that. But very soon this twin logic appeared in the work of the American mathematician and father of cybernetics, Norbert Wiener, who wrote in 1950 that someday it would be possible to "telegraph a human being."[8] That means that a human being is merely

---

[7] Jean-Pierre Changeux, *L'Homme neuronal*. Paris: Fayard, 1983.
[8] Norbert Wiener, *The Human Use of Human Beings*. Boston: Houghton Mifflin, 1950.

a collection of a given quantity of units of information. The latter can be transmitted by means of a neutral medium, different from biological molecules, thus making it possible to reconstruct the individual elsewhere.

The idea that the living being can be modeled in units of information is classical in biology. In particular, it postulates that deoxyribonucleic acid (DNA) is the medium of a code that can be moved to other media. However, when living beings are modeled in units of information, one forgets that the living being is not the sum of these units. We find the same principle in the transhumanist idea of "mind uploading" (the future possibility of uploading a human being—considered as a pure aggregate of data—to a computer).

But where did the idea of reducing the living being to a set of data come from?

Wiener's master stroke, through which he established an idea that still seems obvious today, even though it is unjustified, was to associate energy and information. Since the first decades of the twentieth century, the second law of thermodynamics, according to which the entropy of a system can only increase, fascinated scientists everywhere, as though they had discovered a fundamental truth in the laws of the universe: every system can move only toward more disorder . . . Today, it is hard to understand how this law was a revelation for people back then. Interpretations were excessive: everything is energy, and that energy can only be lost. Claude Shannon, the father of information theory, was already talking about entropy, but Wiener then associated units of energy with units of information. That is what allowed him to say that everything was made up of units of information.[9]

But isn't there a big difference between a unit of energy and a unit of information?

Of course. Energy is a physicochemical measure that can be quantified and modeled, keeping in mind that what is modeled is not the thing itself. On the other hand, if everything is information, then information can be modeled, and everything can be reduced to an algorithm.

Why was this exaggerated association of energy with information established so solidly? Does it have to do with the technological or even technicist worldview that was characteristic of the time?

You could say that. But above all, Shannon, while he was employed by Bell Laboratories in the 1940s, was working on cryptography and the very concrete problems raised by telecommunications at that time, notably those

---

[9] However, it must be noted that Wiener contradicts himself: on the one hand, he constantly associates information with energy; on the other, he asserts, in his book *Cybernetics, or Control and Communication in the Animal and the Machine* (Boston: MIT Press, 1948), that he is a materialist, and that information is not equivalent to energy (Chapter 5, p. 132).

connected with noise. His question was initially an engineer's question: namely, how to improve the coding of a message to transmit it in the most reliable, economical way possible. That was the approach that led him to establish a method for measuring the quantity of information, not of an isolated message, but of its source. In 1948, he published an article that set forth his mathematical theory of communication, in which information is considered independently not only of its medium, but also of any question regarding its meaning. Shannon was not directly interested in the content of messages. His theory was a theory of the code. It was later to undergo spectacular developments. And it did so far beyond engineering-specific problems. It was to be adopted and adapted not only in the domains of telecommunications and computer science, but also in biology, physics, and the human sciences.

But how did we arrive at this misleading association of the neural with the cybernetic?

It is in no way limited to cybernetics. In Descartes's time, it was believed that the organism functioned like a clock. In every period, people have wanted to see technological mechanisms as reflecting the structure of the living being. In the eighteenth century, the age of automatons, humans were seen as automatons. In the age of cybernetics, we see the living being as a circulation of information. This notion is found in many domains, such as neurology, immunology, and cellular biology. Research in these disciplines reveals feedback mechanisms that allow the exchange of information via circuits. Today, biological knowledge is modeled and stored in accord with the rules of computer science.

But isn't knowledge often produced on the basis of analogies? After all, this analogy between the living being and the computer is very practical.

The association between the brain and the wiring of a machine actually begins with the work of Alan Turing and his famous 1950 article entitled "Computing Machinery and Intelligence."[10] However, on this point he very clearly declared that the brain is not a machine with discrete states.

Can the first work on artificial intelligence be connected to the libertarian and ecological trend that arose on the West Coast in the 1960s, some of whose proponents later held key posts in Silicon Valley?

The machine made it possible to reconnect with the axiom of 1900, which said that what is rational is analytically predictable. It promises to make rationality predictable again. But alongside the "serious" research carried on by large companies like IBM, interest in computers was accompanied, rather surprisingly, by a mystical and esoteric

[10] *Mind* 49 (1950), 433–460.

view of the machine. Today we are astonished by transhumanism, which engages in a kind of religious worship of
computer science . . . But, to tell the truth, this esoteric
temptation existed from the outset. In France, for instance,
up until the 1960s, people interested in cybernetics, including Gilles Deleuze and Félix Guattari, saw the computer's
power as very subversive, very profound, possibly revealing
mysteries. And, in fact, cybernetics was, to put it succinctly,
born on the left and overinvested with a magical, liberating
aura, before it took a turn toward the right.

Take the case of the Palo Alto Mental Research
Institute (MRI) in California: it was in this milieu that a
very interesting trend in neurophysiology also appeared,
represented in particular by the works of Francisco Varela,
which have greatly influenced me. It was also there that
the anti-psychiatric movement, to which I adhere, arose. In
Palo Alto, there were anarchist and anti-establishment hip-
pies who were very interested in Buddhist thought and
who carried out research on information theory and cybernetics in the service of individual and collective emancipation: they saw in cybernetic machines a kind of material-
ization of the Buddhist universal spirit, of the great
Buddhist world-consciousness, a consciousness without a
subject. Moreover, it was also at MRI that the anthropolo-
gist Gregory Bateson imagined a theory of communication
articulated around the notion of a network, and in which
the self is absent. All these theories were to bring about the
digitalization of the world. Thus, paradoxically, it was this
milieu that would give rise to Silicon Valley. In the mean-
time, a very important break took place: the digital world

is not the Buddhist universal consciousness that people in Palo Alto dreamed of, but rather a digital governmentality of the world.

How did this change toward the digital governmentality of the world come about?

The researchers in Palo Alto, or their French equivalents, thought they could see in cybernetics a concrete realization of their philosophy, allowing them to free themselves from individualism, the prison of the self, and to reconnect with landscapes and contexts to be able to live within an ecosystem. They did not deny the existence of individuals *qua* individualities but wanted to move beyond this level of surface reality to become aware of the networks we are included in, whether cultural or natural. These ideas led to the theory of emergence: simple, unprogrammed units were supposed to combine to produce something new together. This very fashionable theory sought to explain the evolution of species, the appearance of thought and consciousness. The naive and romantic idea associated with it was that in that way we could liberate ourselves from identity-related attachments.

In France, a philosopher like Gilbert Simondon, a theorist of individuation and networks, can be seen as part of that movement: for him, individuation originates in the "folds" (the person, the landscape, the people . . .) of the network—the term "fold" (*pli*) was, moreover, highly prized by Gilles Deleuze. Reality would thus be the fabric of which cybernetic interaction is made, and from which folds emerge. That is precisely what Buddhist thought says. Hinduism also says that the individual is *maya* (illusion): we are persons and not individuals. Now, in French, the word "personne" can mean "no one," and it also signifies, etymologically, "mask" (Lat. *persona*). The individual is thus a mask with no one behind it, because behind this mask there is only an interconnected network.

That is a conception extremely different from the one we find today in transhumanism!

Without even going so far as transhumanism, all we have to do is consider super-connected "geeks": they are no longer individuals, not because they are becoming persons again but because they have become a profile. The virtual profile of a person is a rather corrupt ersatz for this project of knowing that one is no more than a single element in this vast cybernetic connection. For Deleuze, virtuality had a positive sense: he was talking about virtualities that were possible and emancipatory. Today, the virtuality of a hyperconnected individual is a post-organic, dematerialized world.

Didn't the transition from one world to the other take place in the 1980s?

No doubt it did. It seems to me that the 1980s witnessed the arrival of a major anthropological transition facilitated by digital modeling: with molecular and synthetic biology, we see everything as an accumulation of elementary particles that form a code, which is a specific arrangement of units of information. Living beings are seen as Legos: we ignore the singularity of the living. From the '80s on, synthetic biology has asserted that it is possible to create life *ex nihilo* on other molecular and chemical bases. If everything is information, I can identify precisely the information that characterizes a living being, capture all the data, and reconstruct that living being on other bases. That follows directly from Claude Shannon's information theory: for him, information circulates on a neutral medium. If, as mammals, we are a simple quantity of information that is found in our DNA, then according to synthetic biology, there's no need to attach that information to macromolecules of DNA and proteins . . . Therefore, I can use this information and transfer it to any medium at all, and why not a computer?

Isn't that what most current biologists think?

When I put together a book of interviews with the biologist Pierre-Henri Gouyon,[11] we differed on this question. For Pierre-Henri, DNA is information that circulates on macromolecules. He gave the example of apple pie: I may have the recipe for apple pie on a computer or on paper, or transmit it orally and reproduce it elsewhere, but that does not change the recipe . . . But I disagree: macromolecules

[11] Miguel Benasayag and Pierre-Henri Gouyon, *Fabriquer le vivant?* Paris: La Découverte, 2012.

of DNA are the expression of physicochemical processes that I can model, but for all that, you mustn't confuse the map with the territory! And of course, if we consider works in epigenetics that demonstrate the influence of the environment on gene expression, then yes, these macromolecules of DNA—*qua* physicochemical reality and not as a neutral medium for information—transmit something to the human body. We act "as if," in DNA, there were very distinct forms of genes. Research still uses a methodological reductionism, but that is only one element of scientific work, because holistic science is impossible.

The fact remains that the gene is a model, not reality: it does not exist in a distinct way. To be sure, if I treat a segment of DNA as if it were a gene, that makes different genetic manipulations possible. But this operation is an epistemological banality that implies that we always act according to an operational fiction and not by unveiling truth of some kind. The genetic paradigm is like a map, but it is no more the territory than DNA is. We can use this model because it's powerful, but we must at all costs avoid substantializing it. One of the consequences is that for biologists, all that has to be done is to model the genes, throwing away 90 percent of the DNA that is seen as "non-coding" in the process.

There will probably come a time when we will discover that this 90 percent of DNA considered "useless" performs functions not yet recognized.

No doubt. Consider the case of the brain's glial cells,

which surround the neurons: for a very long time, it was thought that they served no purpose . . . Today we're discovering that they're very useful. So it wasn't that God put padding in the cranium to keep the brain balanced! But the problem isn't limited to a lack of knowledge about certain zones of DNA. It's a more general epistemological problem that the biologist Henri Atlan clearly explained.[12] Every function has a fictional aspect. That doesn't mean that a function is untrue; it means that a function is a fiction that is operative. Thus, its fictional aspect must not be forgotten. For example, I can maintain that the heart is an organ whose function is to pump the blood. That is true, but it doesn't mean it's the heart's only function.

So we have to avoid reducing any organ to a pure function? And thus avoid functionalism?

Exactly. One of my Florentine friends, Stefano Mancuso, is a biologist who works on plants.[13] When we met, he laughed and said he was a "neurophysiologist of plants"! That wording surprised me, as plants don't have brains . . . His works are fascinating: they show that plants, even though they don't have the corresponding organs,

[12] Henri Atlan, *Entre le cristal et la fumée. Essai sur l'organisation du vivant*. Paris: Points, 2018.
[13] Stefano Mancuso, *The Revolutionary Genius of Plants: A New Understanding of Plant Intelligence and Behavior*. New York: Simon and Schuster, 2018; original Italian edition, 2017.

perform functions that the nervous system usually performs. Thus they manage, in their own way, to fulfill the function of vision. This clearly shows, it seems to me, that the modular approach—which consists in thinking that a living being is constructed by fabricating a model that reproduces organs performing functions—is completely false. In fact, the living being integrates relations and not interactions . . . The living being is not a collection of organs that interact; it is a set of organs and tissues that are related to each other. This relation is integrative, so that in the case of living beings, integration is much more important than the organs in themselves.

At the present time, it seems to me that we have a great deal of difficulty conceiving of the living being in terms of interrelated organs.

Marcel Proust said very rightly that "Facts do not find their way into the world in which our beliefs reside" (trans. Scott Moncrieff). Since we believe in cybernetics, the factual reality as Mancuso presents it, even though it is accessible for everyone, is ignored by almost everyone. However, his experiments can be seen on YouTube: he shows how a plant can locate an obstacle without touching it and then develop in such a way as to avoid this obstacle. He also shows that two plants living alongside one another recognize each other and maintain a certain distance between them. He shows the facts phenomenologically, but obviously he does not explain them. The plant is characterized by the fact that it does not have differentiated organs like those of animals. But it performs functions that in an animal would depend on vision, touch, hearing . . . without having the corresponding organs. In particular, he shows that young plants "play": he's using anthropomorphic language that could be criticized, yes, but we can agree with him regarding the fact that playing means experimenting with possibilities.

Why do you say that? How is it related to information theory?

All of this reveals a singularity of the living being. This being functions in accord with a non-modelizable, overall integration, and cannot be cut up into a set of modular functions and organs. I can mentally divide up the living being for practical purposes. But nothing tells me that our Western division of the human body is truer than that of the Chinese, who map it in an entirely different way. In contrast, it corresponds to diverse, non-transposable practices and logics. That is why the idea of the living being as a set of information leaves out a fundamental, vital principle, the principle of integration.

The anthropocentric mode of reasoning, through which the behaviors of other species are overinterpreted on the human model, is present in sociobiology. Edward O. Wilson,[14] for example, attributes to ants various social

[14] Edward O. Wilson, *Sociobiology: The New Synthesis*. Cambridge: Harvard University Press, abridged edition, 1975.

functions, membership in castes (soldiers, workers, etc.), and sees the anthill as a society.

Sociobiological ideas border on the ridiculous with Richard Dawkins's "selfish gene,"[15] according to which the true individual is the gene, which does everything it can to reproduce itself in exactly the same form, whereas we human beings are merely the vehicle. This is a completely metaphysical view that brings to mind the Bible, where it's written that the body is the vehicle of the soul . . . In addition, from a biological point of view, there is no reason to say that the core of the living being is the gene.

Dawkins also bases his view on the idea of the living being as information, writing that the gene seeks to reproduce itself to continue to exist, and thus to replicate the set of information that constitutes it.

Yes, we see that idea again with the principle of the "meme," the elements of cultural information that are replicated in a society. Dawkins draws a very clear distinction between the gene's materiality and memes, utterances such as "Coca-Cola is refreshing" or "Macron is a good president." With that in mind, he de-semanticizes the units of information. For him, neither the living being nor culture has meaning. In his view, the meme goes viral and

---

[15] Richard Dawkins, *The Selfish Gene*. Oxford: Oxford University Press, 1976.

enters into conflict with other memes, which is an absolutely psychotic conception of culture! For example, in 1920s Germany, the little Nazi meme of *Lebensraum* was more virulent than Rosa Luxemburg's "Workers of the world, unite!" And for him, these two memes have no particular meaning. The "victory" of this or that meme/utterance is not explained by any context or any particular signification. He has the same problem as a geneticist that he has as a sociobiologist: in order to accept such a reductionism, he has to abolish 99 percent of the historical, geographical, economic, and ecological context! The same goes for genes: in the film *Jurassic Park* (1993), a mad scientist who has found dinosaur genes succeeds in making them express themselves and recreates a living dinosaur. But in reality, this is impossible, because one gene taken out of its epigenetic context cannot express itself. Today, thanks to the discovery of prions, we know that even a gene's DNA will be changed depending on the context. Thus, neither a gene nor a "meme" can be identically reproduced, as Dawkins thinks it can.

Personally, I think the crazy and even fascistic excesses of sociobiology cast light on the error involved in seeing the living being as a set of units of information, which is also the great error of the theorists of the digital world. The world of information theory, with its new-generation algorithms capable of "learning" through statistical input, of programming themselves, is based on an autonomy of algorithmic combinatorics: it is neither for nor against anything at all but exists outside of any signification. That is why a project of macroeconomic management through AI does

not take into account this or that region, or this or that segment of citizens . . . Many people find Dawkins's theories
ridiculous and understand the absurdity of an asemantic
meme, but in reality, the same asemantic logic is at work in
our vision of a digital world and in that of a macroeconomy
guided by Big Data, which almost no one challenges.

Let's sum up what we've discussed in this first part . . .

After a century of this crisis of rationality, we have seen
that, thanks to cybernetics, we've moved to a new promise
in the postmodern world, or rather in the hypermodern
world, as Michel Foucault called it. In modernity, Man *qua*
human being must fulfill himself by being completely
rational. In hypermodernity, it is the machine that must
achieve this total rationality.

Post-democracy

We have entered a period that is difficult to define at the level of collective action. What do you think, for example, of the "gilet jaunes" (yellow vests) movement in France?

This movement no doubt represents the people who are left out of macroeconomic models: the supernumeraries who have understood that today, the system considers them superfluous. In recent years, Western societies, no matter how developed, have seen the emergence of new, invisible barriers that demarcate new forms of apartheid. The system's supernumeraries suffer in their bodies. That is why these bodies are demonstrating *qua* bodies. They demonstrate in places that represent a gross excess of luxury, comfort, and power. And the savage police repression confirms their terrible suspicion that says, in substance, "Yes, you're going to disappear." In Argentina, during the dictatorship, the military eliminated its opponents by making their bodies disappear. In the Western countries, bodies are not eliminated, but they are asked to suffer in silence and out of sight. Nonetheless, this anger is rising, fanned by governmental repression and the profound incomprehension of the left, a part of which is content to act like

Charlie Chaplin in *Modern Times* when he finds himself carrying a flag at the head of the protest march.

Here we must distinguish between what can be considered the justified anger of the oppressed and its transformation into hatred. Hatred is a mechanism of narcissistic identification of the self with itself that is closed to any conflictuality and to all multiplicity, whereas anger remains one more element in a multiple whole. Unfortunately, the far right is better acquainted with hatred than any other political group.

What do you mean when you speak of post-democracy?

It is very hard to bid farewell to a vision of Man as a messiah and prophet. As a result, we seek, no matter the price, everything that might resemble a messianic popular movement. But this is an outdated quest: we all sense the impotence of this old model of collective action. How should we act, then? It's a real problem. Marx's eleventh thesis on Feuerbach was that "philosophers have hitherto only interpreted the world in various ways; the point is to change it." But "changing the world" is not easy because everyone agrees that rationality has lost its predictive ability. We have understood that we are not able to predict what will happen as a result of our acts. The future is unpredictable, but so is the past, since we cannot predict which parts of the past will be revived, either.

We thought we could act in the modern world: if I want to, I can leave point A to go to point B. Today, we know that we can go to Y or T. It's not that humans cannot do things. But humans realize that their action is part of a whole, including many other elements that are non-human, animal, meteorological, ecological, etc. Humanity understands that human beings are not the only acting subjects of history. Someone who is unaware that he is imbued with the context conceives of himself as a vessel under his control and as the author of his thoughts. In a sort of return from exile, humanity is resituated within nature and reality. The consequences are immense. Action in a human group is at the very least connected with many other vectors, and it is impossible for us to predict the outcome.

Complexity has always existed; it's just that we weren't aware of it before, right? The French Revolution was the result of a large number of variables whose outcome couldn't be predicted in advance.

I wouldn't say that. The irruption of complexity is a major epistemological and historical fact. An act, in itself, isn't something clear. But we can agree that we know what action is. If I act on a political or urban planning issue, I must know that my action will be connected with many other vectors, and that the result is in large measure unforeseeable.

The case of the Revolution is complicated. We can analyze historical situations with the instruments of complexity. I'll give an example: historians have adopted the theory of emergence. They interpret all historical transformations since prehistory as forms of emergence. They believe that the instruments that allow us to interface with the period represent the truth of that period . . . But we have to have the humility and the wisdom to understand that the theories of emergence or of complexity are what allow us to think today, in our period, in more or less rational terms.

Doesn't that reasoning draw from Thomas Kuhn's epistemology?[16] Every period invents its own scientific paradigms that allow it to conceive the world, and these are not transposable to another period.

Yes, that's partly what I mean. I can identify elements of complexity in the time of Galileo's and Newton's theories, but those elements will remain marginal in relation to the theories. Whereas today, in the context of current theories in physics and biology, elements of complexity are central. In Newton's time, people thought in deterministic and linear terms, but their action and their rationality were not therefore "false." We cannot say they were mistaken in not taking into account a core of complexity that they would have refused to see . . . The understanding of reality is a construction that evolves depending on the period, and each period has its own limits. Starting around 1900, it became impossible to think exclusively in Newtonian terms, which are linear and deterministic.

[16] Thomas S. Kuhn, *The Structure of Scientific Revolutions*. Chicago: University of Chicago Press, 1962.

This historical evolution of our understanding of reality also affects the human sciences (history, sociology, anthropology).

That's right. Today, someone who conceives the world in terms of modernity, for example a militant who wants to change the world by identifying classes and sites of power, is acting with an outdated method. We are in fact contemporary with the centrality of complexity. For us, at the clinical, scientific, and political levels, it's impossible to claim complete predictability. We are returning to exactly what Spinoza said.

What did Spinoza say about the difficulty of predicting the result of our actions?

In his time, Spinoza was marginal and a member of a minority. His work was not in synch with the dominant thought of the time, which was Cartesian. He wrote that I cannot foresee the consequence of my act: I can act well, but acting well may lead to evil; conversely, I can act badly, but acting badly may produce a good result. If that is so, how can acts be classified? He proposed to classify them according to their intention, distinguishing between the will to act well and the will to act badly. He imagined the possibility of non-predictability at the time when Galileo, Newton, and Kepler were defining perfect predictability in the sciences. Today, social movements continue to navigate using the outdated maps of predictability, denying the whole territory of current complexity.

Within all these movements, we find the same impossible mourning for human beings' transformative power. The question people ask themselves is, "What should we do?" or "How should we act?" and even "What does action mean today?" . . . The very strong desire, confronted by such questions, is to fabricate a "remake" of the past. We are always looking for providential men or women who could change the world. The fact that we have invented the term "Anthropocene" shows, of course, that humans have changed the world as a whole, but the result is in no way governed by a plan: no one consciously wanted to transform the planet into a gigantic trash bin.

How do you connect this observation about a humanity incapable of predicting the consequences of its own actions to the advent of artificial intelligence?

I connect it because of the catastrophic encounter between digital technology and a humanity disoriented by its lack of control over the world (in the successive catastrophes of Auschwitz, Hiroshima, or again, in a more diffuse way, in the Anthropocene, etc.). Despite rationality, humanity has given rise to monsters like Hitler, Stalin, and Pol Pot. As for technology, we have learned that it can also lead to horrors . . . Nevertheless, up to this point, science and reason have been the two pillars that guided humanity toward a supposed "good" transformation of the world and toward emancipation. Then this humanity disappointed with itself encounters the digital world. With this new utopia, humanity delegates its power to the machine. From now on, people close to the centers of power—economists, bankers—take the death of human beings for granted and deliberately delegate decision-making functions to the machine.

Isn't there a certain cynicism in allowing a machine to decide the fate of stock markets?

No, it's not cynicism. They have understood that they can't control the course of events, and they think the machine can. Consider the Group of Ten, which brought together intellectuals such as Edgar Morin, Michel Rocard, Henri Laborit, Jean Petitot, and Henri Atlan: they postulated that given the technoscientific complexity of our societies, it was not up to officials elected by voters who were almost completely ignorant of all these problems to resolve them. So they proposed, in very Platonic fashion, that scientists henceforth deal with the issues confronting our societies.

But neither Edgar Morin, nor Jean Petitot, nor Michel Rocard adopted a cynical or reactionary position. They noted that democracy doesn't work because complexity has become so extreme that the average person cannot vote in accord with his soul and conscience. Therefore, scientists are the ones who ought to guide major decisions, with the help of machines. Consequently, they then devoted themselves, as Jean Petitot put it, to the *desacralization of the social*. Until the 1960s, the social had been made sacred, and in such a conception of society, humanity was its own messiah and prophet. Man, *qua* subject of history, was to emancipate himself.

But with the eugenics of the 1920s in Britain, Germany, and the United States, and in France with Alexis Carrel (a collaborator with the Vichy regime and a friend of Nazi racial hygienists) and the Sociéte française d'eugénique, we already had this idea of a society governed by scientists, who were supposedly the only ones suited to perform that role.

Of course, the fantasy of a society governed by scientists is even older; it can be traced back to Malthusianism or even to Plato, who, in his *Republic*, proposed to make philosophers the king's councilors. But what I especially wanted to say was that modernity desacralizes God in order to sacralize Man. The additional step taken today is the desacralization of the social, meaning, if we read very carefully what the Group of Ten says,[17] that the ordinary individual cannot know anything about complex mechanisms. Beyond the apparent scorn, this is a problem that must be taken seriously. I discussed this at length with certain intellectuals when the question of nanotechnologies emerged as a subject of public debate. My argument was the following: a very serious gentleman wearing a tie approaches us and says that nanotechnologies are the solution to all our problems. Another fellow, more relaxed and agreeable, comes in and explains in turn that nanotechnologies are evil. With lectures like these, how can the

[17] Cf. Miguel Benasayag (with Angélique Del Rey), *De l'engagement dans une époque obscure*. Paris: Le Passager clandestin, 2011.

public at large form a precise opinion on the question? The same goes for GMOs: an ecologist can explain how bad he thinks they are, and a Hindu can explain that, thanks to them, he can finally eat his fill. Confronted by these differing views, the ordinary citizen is expected to believe in this or that explanation.

One might even add that this crisis of belief, this doubt regarding what we should think, also affects scientists. Many of them do not know exactly what they should think, even concerning their own subject.

Absolutely, and that is why I completely disagree with this argument. But what matters most is understanding that the idea of entrusting decisions to the machine doesn't come from ignorant billionaires, but rather from scientists who have reflected on the question, and that is much more serious. The result, whatever one thinks of it, is that a tiny minority of humanity has deliberately delegated decisions to machines. Of course, most of humanity accepts this decision without having any voice in it, and even without being aware of it. If I use my GPS to go to a certain place in my car, I don't think about the fact that I am delegating a whole set of cognitive functions to the machine.

Nevertheless, it's a fact: cab drivers in London find their own way, whereas Parisians systematically use their GPS. Measurements of cerebral imagery have shown that after a year, the subcortical centers that map time and space have atrophied in the Parisian cab drivers. Of course, this atrophy can be reversed if the person involved gives up this practice . . . However that may be, the drivers were affected by a kind of dyslexia that diminished their ability to orient themselves in time and space. This example illustrates one of the neurological consequences of delegating cerebral functions to machines.

Confronted by this bleak picture of humanity's delegation of decisions to machines, what do you propose?

Today, people are saying that we must "re-politicize" the social field. But it is physically impossible to return to the world of the past. In the old days, people proposed storming the Winter Palace. But now, there is no longer a czar who enjoys the serfs' suffering . . . And even though it might seem desirable to overthrow the offices of IBM or Google, doing so would change nothing! In the present system, almost everyone is incorporated, willingly or not. Knowing that human beings, already largely broken up and colonized by the machine, cannot control their actions, we have to redefine new units of action.

But what characterizes post-democracy?

I think modern democracy has to be distinguished from the stereotype with which it's often compared, namely democracy as the rule of the majority. For me, what constitutes democracy is the existence of tolerance and conflictuality. Let's take the question of the majority: in Greek democracy, two free men won out over another free man because they were more numerous—and then there were the slaves, who had no voice in the matter. But even if they won, they had to come to terms with the laws that were already in place. That's what democracy is: I have to come to terms, in a conflictual way, with the Other. That is one of the differences between democracy and dictatorship: in dictatorship or totalitarianism, otherness appears as an undesirable accident that has to be eliminated. There is no conflictuality, only oppositions that must be done away with; our current democracies tend toward this model. Moreover, we are witnessing the emergence of the question of cultural identity, which goes hand in hand with the disappearance of a common base.

But isn't the question of cultural identity more complex? Take the case of minorities who assert their identity to be better recognized in the public sphere.

Humanism, which is challenged today, proposed an abstract universal as the foundation of society. Against those who said that some people were less human than others, it asserted, "All people are human." One of the consequences of the break with modernity is the collapse of this single foundation and the appearance of cultural relativism, in which confrontation becomes the primary relationship with the Other. Today's alliances are more easily made by sharing hatred than by seeking common ground.

Does cultural relativism have to lead to hate? Claude Lévi-Strauss, the eulogist of cultural relativism, defended,

on the contrary, "a third type of humanism"[18] (after the humanism of the Renaissance and bourgeois humanism) that would take into account both the rights of minorities and the rights of animals. He advocated cultural relativism for small minorities, such as the Amerindians, living in remote areas and threatened with extinction by colonialism and imperialism.

Lévi-Strauss appeared in a particular context: he developed his thought in opposition to his predecessors who, like Lucien Lévy-Bruhl, maintained that "primitive peoples" had a prelogical way of thinking. Lévi-Strauss, in contrast, reintegrates these non-Western peoples by emphasizing the logic of their thought and their full-fledged membership in a common humanity. For me, in concrete terms, even though he's defending cultural relativism to safeguard endangered cultures, Lévi-Strauss nonetheless remains in a universalist logic, even if he gives it a new form.

The basis of universalism was questionable because it also gave rise to colonialism and racism. However that may be, we are moving beyond universalism, which has been replaced by cultural relativism, a concept that in France is appealed to by both minorities and the far right since Alain de Benoist and the New Right used it to reform their ideological apparatus.

[18] Claude Lévi-Strauss, *Anthropologie structurale deux*. Paris: Plon, 1973.

Pierre-André Taguieff's analyses,[19] which are already rather old, would suggest that Alain de Benoist is even the theorist of cultural differentialism, an extreme form of cultural relativism that completely rejects the Other and seeks to keep cultures hermetically sealed off from one another.

What is dangerous are the excesses of cultural relativism, which lead both to the differentialism of a Benoist and to an individualist ultra-relativism that asserts that we all have their own truth. Grand ideals connected with grand narratives have been replaced by petty narratives that begin, "As for me, I . . .": what I do in my life is intended only to serve my own interests and my own pleasure. History no longer has a direction and a meaning, there is no longer any progress of humanity, no longer any narrative of emancipation . . . Instead of a common hope, there remains only a wretched little ideal of individual happiness. As a clinician, I see this very clearly, because that is what my patients tell me: people don't feel the ties within their romantic relationships, with their children or their parents, as an ontological bond; they experience them as an optional bond, the choice depending on their personal pleasure and interest.

This individualism in which we all choose our relationships with others in the interest of our personal pleasure alone is truly frightening.

[19] Pierre-André Taguieff, *La Force du préjugé. Essai sur le racisme et ses doubles*. Paris: La Découverte, 1988.

It's nothing less than barbarism. We are living in an era of hypernominalism in which the ties between human beings are experienced as purely imaginary. That goes very well with neoliberalism, which destroys all ties and deterritorializes everything.

What impact does AI have on this ultra-relativist and individualist world that you're describing?

The society controlled by AI is presented to us as a kind of aristocracy without aristocrats. In fact, the machine no longer has any boss. We are told that it suffices to unplug the machine to stop its functioning, but that's illusory. Moreover, the machine adapts to situations, whereas the living being does not: the living being is neither adaptive nor autonomous but coevolves within the bundle of ties it's made of.

People seek to predict the future as if it were unforeseeable, but what is most unforeseeable is in reality the past: when Pierre lives through a day, all the stimuli that he experiences (the subway, the boss . . .) interfere with the great mass of his memories, such as traumas, habits, etc., that come from his history, that of his parents, of his milieu, and even of his species. From a clinical point of view, the present moment occupies hardly 10 to 15 percent of our thoughts. Even so, we cannot foresee what part of the past will be revived in our present; in a given situation, it may lay a trap for us or, on the contrary, save the day. In a subway car, contrary to AI, which would be 100 percent present, hardly 10 to 15 percent of each of us is really present. Individuals exist

90 percent within their own film connected with their past. What is characteristic of humans is therefore the unpredictability of both the past and the future, as well as the aleatory nature of the present. This creates reflexes, but also waves of impulses. Conversely, AI appears to be completely reliable. That is why humanity has massively delegated its functions—for example, in stock markets—to this extremely powerful machinery that is here to stay, perhaps forever.

For many leaders, it seems reassuring that a machine can in theory predict everything.

Yes, but that means forgetting that what is peculiar to life is that it's caught up in the complex entanglement of the past, present, and future, which is no way programmable. Today, AI fabricates models for the economy, but also for urban planning. Take the case of vehicular traffic. When I was studying questions of uncertainty in mathematical logic twenty years ago, I had an opportunity to work at the University of Jussieu in Alain Cardon's laboratory, and I noted that the "ideal" model of uncertainty and indetermination researchers were using was vehicular traffic.

However, there are applications for smart phones that are supposed to predict the ideal route for a car and are supposedly based on algorithms that model vehicular traffic . . . So it might be asked what these applications "predict."

Right, that's the question. The act of driving with the aid of a machine allegedly transforms reality by making it more rational. But the act aided by the machine merely adds an additional layer of complexity!

Let's move on to another aspect of what you call "post-democracy." Doesn't a permanent relationship to the digital world, the internet connection, imply a loss of the subject's concentration, as several recent studies claim?

In the epoch of Man, democracy was based on the sacralization of the social. Today, the social and human beings are no longer sacred. The prohibition against touching the body was a good example of the sacralization of Man. When I arrived in France in the early 1980s, I was surprised to see the propaganda of dictatorships on the news, denying that they engaged in torture. In the epoch of Man, the human body was untouchable, except by physicians, who touch the body in a de-subjectivized way, in the same way that a priest has the right to touch sacred objects. But that era is over. Torture is openly acknowledged today, bodies are touched and manipulated in a desacralized way, and that is what the transhumanists propose with their vision of the human being enhanced to make a "bionic man." The time when the human being was sacred is over. In our liberal and technological democracies, the most insignificant demonstrator can be violently attacked and lose an eye or a hand.

What impact does the desacralization of Man have on democracy?

For me, the distinction between functioning and existing

is essential: the living being exists, in contrast to the machine, which merely functions. Now, a distinction of that kind tends to become obsolete: for science, bodies function, but they exist less and less. This desacralization has another consequence: democracy was the institution in which humanity, in its sacred nature, elected its representatives to transform the world. Today, this desacralized humanity retains democratic rituals, but its institutions are themselves desacralized, and so are the political leaders—with the exception of preachers of hate like Salvini in Italy or Bolsonaro in Brazil. That's what the post-democratic era is. Human beings, who have lost their sacred character, have delegated their power of action to machines. No matter whom we vote for, machines decide what to do. Neither is it a matter of a sadist deciding to create an "economic plan" and cause large numbers of people to lose their jobs: it is still the machine that analyzes the data and deduces that employees have to be fired . . . In the current macroeconomic model, almost no one questions this growing delegation of decision-making to machines.

How do people react when confronted by post-democracy?

Currently, we are witnessing two types of responses: on the one hand, a movement of total deception and, on the other, a temptation to return to the past, to repoliticize the questions that are now handled by machines. But instead, we have to invent new forms of action that can counterbalance the activity of a small group of scientists like the

Group of Ten. There is no reason why a scientist would be better trained than anyone else to know what would be "good" for the people. And to top it all off, the scientist who created the machine will not control it any more than the technician does. Despite Morin's and Petitot's demands that humans continue to guide the machine, today we have to admit that the contrary is true: humans have become the servants of the machine. Thus, the *Republic*'s Platonic wish is now outdated.

The consequences of the delegation of politics to AI, some of which have already come to pass, are worrisome. For example, the "predictive" detection of potentially dangerous behaviors based on analysis of video surveillance (in use in China and Israel and tested in Paris, in the Châtelet-Les Halles subway station).

There is also the "Patriot Act" in the United States, which allows the government to listen in on telephone conversations and analyze them using AI, on the basis of keywords. And there is the Chinese project of analyzing, based on models of recognition, all aspects of citizens' behavior, and giving them a social grade . . . AI, beyond this terrifying "Big Data" aspect, is increasingly present in our lives—for example, in medicine, where some diagnoses of skin cancer are made by the machine. But what is essential to understand is that with this importance accorded to AI, we are once again losing a little more faith in human reason and granting total credibility to the machine, which doesn't make mistakes.

" In a world subject
to digital governance,
the body is a stubborn
obstacle. "

How does AI manage bodies?

That's the question. If we except transhumanist ideology, which would like to rid itself of bodies, the creators of the digital world seek in general to include bodies, trying to "manage" them in a dematerialized way. In a world subject to digital governance, the body is a stubborn obstacle, but everything is done to measure and incorporate it into the digital world. That said, what the most radical transhumanists have in common with any manager of the digital world is a "post-organic" worldview.

Players of the online game "Second Life" (in which an avatar of the player is supposed to live an alternative, purely digital life), who enter into contact with people through the internet, who connect their bodies to various kinds of monitors to measure their effort or their cardiac rhythm, to count the number of steps they take in a day, etc., find themselves, even in a very playful way, caught up in post-organic practices. This type of behavior seeks to do away with any form of "negativity": by living in the digital world, one disciplines one's body in accord with items of "pure positivity" that bring life closer to the side of pure functioning, setting aside one's existence. In the digital world, being is a way of "de-existing." The body is still present, but it is subject to an immaterial regime.

This delegation of politics to the machine, which is voluntary but doesn't control the consequences, is concomitant

with the rise in power of GAFA[20], which today have more power than many nations.

GAFA's increased power doesn't eliminate traditional politics, but it relativizes them . . . It's not a matter of making a *tabula rasa* of the old politics. In fact, mayors, ministers, representatives, presidents, and political parties continue to exist. But they are no longer the authority that guides politics; they are a simple variable in a system that is becoming more and more complex. Thinking about post-democracy and the post-political signifies that there is no longer any immediate, linear relation between what politicians want to do and what they actually will do. I would even say that today, in politics (and this also holds for petitions, demonstrations, citizen initiatives, etc.), when an action has a result that matches expectations, that is due in large measure to chance! That's difficult to accept, but it is the current reality. I can see that certain acts are realized, and it's a good thing! But at the overall level of a society or the planet, we don't have the slightest idea of the consequences of our actions.

It seems to me that everyone is vaguely aware of the fact that we do not control the results of our acts at the global level, and that engenders great anxiety among our contemporaries (an anxiety that did not exist fifty years ago).

That's very probable. Many people are amused by the

---

[20] The Big Four tech companies (Google, Apple, Facebook, Amazon).

idea or choose not to face up to it, while others, like the transhumanists, accept it as inevitable, seeing it as the meaning of history, and even a stroke of luck. For them, the time has come to step down. We find the same reactions with regard to delegating decisions to the machine. When the defenders of transhumanism are told that the brain is being simplified because AI has taken over many cognitive tasks, they accept this as inevitable. In France, Laurent Alexandre, for example—the best-known promotor of transhumanism—is absolutely delighted by it.

How is it possible to be delighted about that?

Humans have delegated throughout history. Since the 1980s, most people have even seen democracy as a way to get out of having to think about situations because they have voted. That is why it is ridiculous to count on being able to export so-called democratic institutions to non-Western countries. Imagine that we want to export democracy to Iraq: you will find Sunnites, Shiites, Kurds, and other parties. Can you imagine a Shiite man studying a Sunnite's political program to see if it might suit him? That would be ridiculous. But if we think about it carefully, we can say exactly the same thing about our Western individualist societies! Most people vote as they are told to, by a sort of inertia. To conclude on post-democracy, we understand today to what point democracy is a myth that is collapsing. Even the idea of an individual, rational citizen is a myth. That is why we have to revamp our way of seeing political action. We have to rethink what it means to act.

THE THEORY OF ACTION

Confronted with this terrible recognition of the machine's colonization of the living being and the delegation of decisions to AI, what sorts of possibilities do we have for acting differently?

To approach the question of action, we have to take into account a central element. We have to admit the reality of algorithmic governmentality—the fact that the life of individuals and societies is guided and structured by machines. But the algorithmic world is neither for nor against the living being; it is indifferent to it. For example, many magistrates in France are worried about the possibility that we're headed for algorithmic tribunals; they would like to continue making decisions based on their souls and consciences. However, AI increasingly assists them in collecting data, making cases, and listing precedents . . . Algorithmic aid is thus already a reality in magistrates' work. The greatest danger, in my opinion, is predictive justice, which claims to identify the danger posed by an individual based on an analysis of a set of micro-data or micro-behaviors. The slightest criminal record could then be taken into account by algorithms. I am referring here to micro-behaviors: it's not that someone has searched the internet to find out how bombs are made! It's much more subtle than that: the machine analyzes micro-interests—purchases online, websites visited, etc.—and, by correlation, it "decides" whether a person is dangerous or is not.

I'll give you an example: Google has set up a system of observation such that when someone uses a credit card for a year, it is able to predict with 85 percent certainty whether that person will get divorced within the next three years . . . Algorithms function on the basis of this micro-information that is collected *en masse* in the digital world, and which, brought together and correlated, determines profiles.

It seems to me that that's the danger of the notion of behavior, which imposes repetitive routines on a life that is far more aleatory than the set of these routines makes it seem.

Yes, but it's not entirely the issue of behavior that's at stake here. My point is the following: objectively, the machine compiles micro-behaviors that might be designated as pre-individual, which are a set of digital traces, habits, regularities, fragments of activity that have nothing to do with the result of the interpretation. In the case of certain illnesses, we want to identify correlations to establish a preventative medicine, but based on these data, which very often have no relationship to the person's health!

The epistemological model on which this governmentality is based is that of the modular human being; it is similar to the one proposed by molecular biology. Individuals are reduced, not to their decisions, but to their micro-behaviors. Biology is not interested in life itself; it is only interested in the elementary particles that associate with each other. The same holds in the case of algorithmic governmentality; if we input a very large number of the most varied micro-acts—where people take their vacations, which route they take, what websites they visit, whom they call, etc.—then it is possible to construct virtual profiles that are supposed to expose dangerous or deviant individuals. Governmentality is therefore no longer addressed to a specific person (even if the notion of "person," as it was used in the former model of governmentality to mean someone who votes his or her soul and conscience, was just as debatable). All the data collected are pre-individual, because persons are assimilated and assimilate themselves to their profiles. There is no meaning. That is exactly the same idea that we find in Richard Dawkins's memes.

So it is a digital view of the person?

Absolutely, advocates of AI are convinced that individuals are machines, that they are the reptacles of various micro-behaviors, without there being any overall meaning. There are no longer any individuals, populations, or communities; there are only profiles, virtual avatars. Algorithms are based on discerning tendencies: for example, whether an individual is potentially violent or not.

From this point on, how can people act in a society that is subject to algorithmic governmentality?

At present, the French government is applying the European Union's economic rules, which are based on models that all share the belief that the world is information. And obviously, the discrete data they use only justify this belief and the economic hypotheses that accompany it. As the mathematician René Thom writes, behind every quantitative model, there is a qualitative hypothesis. However, there are "holes" in this model: they are the millions of French men and women who are watching their standard of living deteriorating. Never mind, new data will be added to the machine that will take that into account. This is very different from General de Gaulle addressing a crowd in Algiers and saying: *"Je vous ai compris . . ."* Here, there is a petty technocrat who implements the model and acts in conformity with the machine's decisions as it decrees what is possible and what is not on the economic level, and what the consequences for the people are. The technocrat calls the fact that he or she is conforming to a machine's orders "realism"—a machine that decrees, for example, the possibility of closing a maternity ward for reasons of economic efficiency. You see the paradox: the machine's abstract decision becomes more real than the reality of a woman who has to travel 200 kilometers to give birth! The problem is that there is no one against whom one can revolt, because it's a robot that makes the decisions—even if the latter always benefit certain persons. In this new context, the politicians in power are no one, they might as well be holograms; that would change nothing at all.

In Philip K. Dick's novel, *The Penultimate Truth*,[21] humans live in underground bunkers and listen on giant screens to their leader, Talbot Yancy. In reality, Yancy is a robot controlled by artificial intelligence, to which false information is given so that it will construct a reassuring discourse . . . In a sense, this author has foreseen our current reality.

Yes, it's a story inspired by a novel by the Argentine author Adolfo Bioy Casares that dates from 1940, *The Invention of Morel*.[22] In any case, the question of action arises. The institution is not facing people who contest it; it is facing movements of micro-behaviors that must be controlled. There is no recognition of conflictuality because the machine eliminates the Other. The slightest criticism is interpreted as a failure that must be either adjusted or eradicated by confronting and repressing it. In every case, if the reactions to the government's policies are not good, that is not because of an ideological disagreement; it's simply because the communication was badly handled, because the memes used were not the right ones. So I use the term post-democracy, because in such a context one can vote

[21] New York: Leisure Books, 1964.
[22] Translation by Ruth L.C. Simms, 1964; rpt. New York: NYRB Classics, 2003.

only for people who have the same program. Moreover, even Matteo Salvini, who openly adheres to Italian fascism, is in reality following the guidance of the European Bank . . . In France, President Emmanuel Macron says he's interested in France's colonial responsibilities, but with regard to migrants, he is doing reluctantly what Madame Le Pen would do with pleasure!

So the conflict necessary for democracy no longer exists?

The question is how we should fight the erasure of otherness. De Gaulle had genuine adversaries: the Americans and the Communists. In Argentina, the military junta had an ideology that it was determined to defend against the revolutionaries. Some military men who were torturing prisoners loved to come in between sessions and explain to them—especially if they were intellectuals—why their battle was important. Today, otherness is no longer taken into account: people claim that terrorists become radicalized for psychological reasons alone. When judges came to ask my opinion concerning deradicalization, I answered that the ideological variable might also have to be taken into account, instead of seeing the matter as a mere symptom. Today, *gilet jaune* protesters are treated the same way: they are delegitimated by reducing them to a set of symptoms to be treated. The conclusion is that no conflict is tolerated, only confrontation is sought. The Other is a barbarian, and against barbarians only barbarity can be used.

I think of those killers who call themselves jihadists,

like the one at the Christmas market in Strasbourg who was killed by the police . . . Many people found that acceptable, whereas it would have more closely resembled justice to arrest him and put him on trial.

Yes, that also reminds me of something Manuel Valls[23] said in 2016: "To explain is already to excuse a bit." I believe that the jihadist phenomenon is a symptom of a radicalization that exists on both sides. On the one hand, we have a West that dreams of humanity in super-individualist, post-organic terms, and explains that there is no limit (our bodies can be cobbled together like Lego structures, we can become immortal, clone ourselves, upload ourselves to a computer, etc.); on the other hand, we have various forms of religious fundamentalism that cling to the supposedly natural values of the human being and the community. In my view, these are two irrational fundamentalisms at war with one another. But it is nonetheless a false opposition that in reality concerns only a very small part of society. However, in the name of these two extremes, all possibility of conflictuality is eliminated.

How is the absence of conflictuality in our societies related to AI?

The application of a "zero tolerance" policy with regard to conflictuality is reinforced by the machine. The latter is

[23] Prime minister of France from 2014 to 2016.

seen as strictly just, but humans are never strictly just! By definition, a machine cannot understand "fuzzy logic": it can calculate that 4 is twice 2, but it cannot know, for example, whether an apartment is "large," because what is it "large" in relation to? In the living being there is a dimension of subjectivity that escapes the machine. Similarly, at the juridical level, a machine cannot take into account what is "legitimate" for a society—but this legitimacy is the cement that holds society together. But the legitimate is not the legal, and if the legitimate is reduced to the legal, life in society becomes unbearable. The real problem with algorithmic governmentality is not that the machine might stop working properly but instead that it determines social orientations that are unbearable, with no loopholes. If a judge is confronted by someone who has stolen in a supermarket, apart from what this individual has stolen, the judge will take into account numerous other elements, such as her poverty. In her decision, she will take this person's biography and subjectivity under consideration. Her decision will recognize that her knowledge is incomplete, because in every reprehensible act, there remain points that are unclear. The machine, however, cannot take all that into account.

But how, then, can we act?

As we have seen, in view of the crisis of societies and cultures, algorithmic governmentality has led us to delegate human rationality to the machine. In this new context, action is compromised. In addition, we're facing a catastrophic situation on the economic, demographic, and ecological levels.

Moreover, if we think in terms of complex systems, we realize that human beings are not the only actors in the world. Heisenberg said that no matter where Man looks, he sees nothing but Man . . . In reality, that's not true. Human action has to reckon with many other active elements that are not human. All human action, in politics or in medicine, must take into account that intentional action is only one vector in a set of other, non-countable vectors, whose regulation is not foreseeable. Nature will regulate itself, perhaps, but humans may no longer be there to witness it!

It's not easy to stay hopeful in that world.

Yes, the question arises as to how to live in a world without promises or even the idea of providence. The idea of providence presupposes that we see evil, even in its worst form, and that although we don't understand it, we believe that all this will lead us to a higher good that will win out. Modernity has produced its own version of providence: teleology, one of whose forms is historicism. Teleology supposes an ascendant dialectic and a goal that will resolve the problems encountered along the way. Today, the novelty is that we have neither providence, nor teleology, nor promises.

But what is it about our time that prevents us from thinking about our way of acting on the world?

We have shifted into a new era, in which our usual manner of acting no longer works. Complexity has become dominant almost everywhere. Let me give an example of an action in complexity: the case of antibiotics. This type of medication was created within a dominant, linear model of the living being. The idea was that there are pathogenic agents and other agents that strengthen the immune system, which is seen as a fortress allowing humans to fight invaders. To a certain extent, that's true. But antibiotics are used *en masse* by groups and individuals; their effects are iatrogenic, and they weaken the body's immune system. But this detrimental effect of antibiotics was not foreseen, which shows that we can no longer conceive of our action in terms of a cause and an effect relative to the cause. Today's science is no longer a science limited to exactitude. It has to be able to cope with a certain level of uncertainty.

However, in our everyday life, everything still seems to confirm the current validity of the old rationality and the existence of linear systems. If I take the subway, I am very likely to arrive at the place where I intended to go. But although certain levels of reality still function in the linear mode (the level of perceptible reality, connected with geometric space and our corporeality), that is no longer the case for other levels. In fact, at the level of "non-immediate" information, we're inundated by data, without being able to determine a result with certainty. Someone who is smoking is not thereby developing cancer. But experience shows that there is a correlation between smoking on a daily basis and developing cancer. What will happen to this person in the future: will she contract cancer? Today, we're confronted by the temptation and excess of managing risks through control by digital technologies, whose pseudo-rational language is about as rational as that of any fortune-teller. The great challenge we face today is to understand this complexity at the level of public health, ecology, demography, and economics.

Here we return to the problem of the Anthropocene, an emerging field of research at the intersection of the most diverse sciences, whose objective is to provide tools for thinking about deregulation and ecological enthusiasm on the planetary level.

That's a good example. To clarify what I'm saying, I will distinguish the domain of the immediate from that of the "mediated," the non-immediate. If I see a sheep afflicted with flatulence, that's immediate. But thinking that a large group of sheep in Australia will cause a hole in the ozone layer is mediated. The problem resides in the fact that in our very disciplinary societies, we don't directly experience what threatens us. I would even say that we can never perceive immediately what threatens us. The perception of complexity requires the possibility of living in a situational time that's not trapped in the immediate. Everything in the apparently very playful technology that captures our everyday life 24/7 pushes us into the immediate. It has to be recognized that, from a clinical point of view, behaviors of addiction to interactions with various digital tools constitute a serious pathology that distances the patient from herself. She loses the ability to have an integrated proprioceptive perception, which leads her toward dislocated functioning. Because the humanity of the digital world is

also the humanity of ultra-feedback and permanent immediacy, we can understand a primary reason for our contemporaries' lack of reaction when confronted by dangers that
are not only outside the realm of immediacy and feedback,
but also require a complex perception of mediated phe-
nomena. Most of our contemporaries are incited to live
elsewhere, but in an elsewhere that is, in reality, nowhere.
And as one can easily imagine, it is very hard to act from
nowhere.

> Whatever I do,
> I cannot control what
> is going to happen.

But today, do we nonetheless have the possibility to act at the individual and collective levels?

Let's go back to Spinoza, who analyzes the fact that I cannot foresee all the consequences of my actions. Sometimes I can act well, but it causes something bad. Inversely, sometimes I act badly, and that causes something good. That's why the level of intentionality occupies such a central place in his thought. Today, Spinoza's reflection concerns everyone, which was not the case in his own time. Whatever I do, I cannot control what is going to happen. Impotence and paralysis are now experienced by everyone: when I am treated as a pure virtual profile, when I feel powerless about the ecological dangers that threaten the planet . . . The general consequence is either that we do not act, or that our action is a desperate confrontation. Personally, I don't think that we will succeed in transcending the difficulties at a global level in our time. In my opinion, the solutions can only be singular: that is, neither wholly local nor solely global, but beyond that dichotomy.

What do you mean by "singular solutions"?

Let's imagine that a large number of humans are capable of attacking global problems rationally. That's not impossible, but even in that case, the reality of complexity means that they won't be able to foresee the consequences of their actions. That is why we have no choice: we must abandon any idea of an overall transcendence of the current problems and imagine another idea of society, of freedom, of justice. All of that has now become impossible. Accepting it and saying farewell to it without giving in to cynicism or to depression requires immense courage. We have to abandon all promise of a future. We have to act in a more unique way, that is, by basing ourselves on the intensive dimension of experiences of resistance/creation, momentarily setting the broader question to one side.

In Argentina, I participated in groups that were applying such a logic. Alongside Marxist groups that were fighting in the name of a radiant future, there was a silent majority that was fighting the dictatorship in the here and now. I was part of that majority: we immanently maintained that the injustice was unacceptable. Later on, I discussed this with Bastien Cany and other friends from the Collectif Malgré Tout[24] in the context of the difference between commitment/revelation and commitment/expression. Commitment/revelation is peculiar to the prophet, the leader, the sad activists who think they recognize in the signs of the present a message from a beyond, in the name of which they assign themselves the role of guiding the masses. In commitment/expression, we act on the basis of shared, objective observation and not through adherence to any kind of program or promise.

[24] A group created by Miguel Benasayag and others with the goal of "connecting the recognition of the complexity of the real with concrete practices of emancipation".

Didn't you have an ideal of democracy to be restored?

Aside from a few political leaders in the resistance, most of the fighters, including those with important military responsibilities, actually only had a very vague ideal. Mine was closer to the advent of the *Era de Acuario* (Age of Aquarius) than to Fidel Castro's Committee to Defend the Revolution. Our motivation was very concrete: we didn't need to believe; we just knew what we didn't want. This experience helps me think about our time. We have to give up any hope of an overall solution. On the contrary, we have to find immanent motivations. In addition, we have to fight to establish a conflictual multiplicity. The protesters at Notre-Dame-des-Landes[25] are a textbook case: they created an extremely localized group including humans, trees, animals, etc., in which the humans were neither the subjects nor the goal. That is also the case for Cédric Herrou, a farmer who is not motivated by great ideas of the future but has simply decided that police treatment of migrants is unacceptable. He acts in the here and now. This reminds me of Samuel Becket's *Waiting for Godot*, in which a fat man falls to the ground and calls for help. Two men witness the scene, and one of them says to the other: "He's calling for help." Later on, the other man says, "To all mankind they were addressed, those cries for help still ringing in our ears! But at this place, at this moment of time, all mankind is us." That is what is called, in philosophy, a concrete universal, a singularity.

[25] See https://en.wikipedia.org/wiki/Notre-Dame-des-Landes.

So you're not advocating for a profound change of the political system?

I don't share the anti-democratic positions of certain far-left thinkers; I don't think the current model has to be attacked head-on. It's fashionable to advocate a *tabula rasa*. But I choose to be less fashionable: in my view, we have to democratize democracy, re-establish conflictuality. That doesn't mean that everyone has to be a local activist like those at Notre-Dame-des-Landes, even if, obviously, they provide a genuine example of active democracy, that is, of a moment at which people get involved, by putting their bodies at stake, in what concerns them. This is a major example, among others, that allows us to recreate conflictuality, to invent active multiplicities. As for me, I'm doing theoretical work to explain how digital modeling cannot exhaust the complexity of the living being: that's another way of situating myself in active multiplicities.

In 1941, my grandfather Joseph locked up his apartment in Paris and, taking his whole family with him, headed for the Free Zone and then Spain and Portugal, finally ending up in Uruguay. I sometimes wonder if we're in a situation comparable to my grandfather's: faced with danger, must we act immediately? Except that in the current case, there is nowhere else to go. That's why we have to be wary of the temptation to become fascinated by the threat, because today, action requires us to assume a great complexity.

The "collapsologists," people influenced by the essayist Pablo Servigne,[26] think that the end of techno-industrial civilization will come in 2045, that it is ineluctable and must be welcomed with open arms. They make a curious mixture of interesting popularization and an astonishing morality, simultaneously catastrophist and redemptive.

I think again of my grandfather Joseph, who left a very short time before the police came to his home: his decision to leave saved his life and the lives of his family. So I say to myself that, like him, we have to take the gravity of the situation to heart. We must avoid denying the gravity of the current situation, taking pleasure in catastrophe like the collapsologists, or like a character in the Tintin book *The Shooting Star*, posing as prophets.

For Servigne, it's not enough to imagine the possibility of catastrophe; we have to be "certain," because if we are certain, we'll be better able to face it. Isn't this reasoning self-contradictory, even absurd?

I consider it a sophism. Rather than being "certain," we should be aware of the fact that we don't know what's going to happen. It's that not-knowing that we have to face. In any critical situation, we never know if the information we have is sufficient to justify action. Because in reality,

---

[26] Pablo Servigne and Raphaël Stevens, *Comment tout peut s'effondrer*. Paris: Le Seuil, 2015.

action is always structured by a wager and not by a point of view that claims to be exact and adequate. Exact and adequate action always produces political commissars and leaders who deprive us of freedoms and prevent the development of a conflictual multiplicity of action. Jean-Paul Sartre wrote somewhere, "We always make commitments with a certain degree of ignorance."

But how can we act concretely and in a situational way against the omnipotence of the machine?

In my view, situational action against the colonization of the living being by the machine—and not against the machine itself—has to be transgressive. We must develop sites of dysfunctionality, and I entrust that to the younger generations, who were born along with the digital world. A certain way of using the machine has colonized us, and now it's up to us to construct experiences and practices of hybridization with technology that respect the singularity of the living being and of culture.

So you don't favor a shrinking world that seeks a complete separation of humanity from the machine?

Actually, while I agree with the objective of degrowth, I do not adhere to the classical idea, inspired by science fiction, according to which we must gain access to the heart of the machine and destroy it. In Brussels, I attended an excellent exposition entitled "My Father, the Robot," at which I had an opportunity to talk about the hybridization of humans and machines. A young man asked me why I was talking about hybridization as a fact. I replied that we have to prefer being hybridized with the machine to being colonized by it. I think hybridization is a fact. The living being is already hybridized with the machine, and it will certainly be hybridized with future products issuing from new technologies.

There are numerous machines that we work with and to which we delegate a certain number of functions. Are they all necessary? That's the question. Above all, we must take care that hybridization respects the living being and culture.

We spend an enormous amount of time orienting ourselves among the various possibilities offered by computers and the internet.

I return to the case of taxi drivers in Paris and London and their use or avoidance of GPS. I've been accused of not liking GPS, as if I like getting lost in the suburbs without the help of that machine. But really, we come back to the distinction between the immediate and the mediated. In the immediate, GPS does in fact allow me to go from point A to point B, and that's very practical; but in the mediated, this use of the machine has potentially disastrous consequences for my brain and for culture. The goal is to have experiences that connect the immediate with the mediated. It's not impossible: for example, today, smokers have succeeded in broadening their field of immediate perception to include the mediated aspect of smoking (the long-term danger of dying as a result). That said, we also have to take into account addiction, which is even more visible in drug users, who in general are completely aware that they're risking death. Thus, we see the limits of reasoning and the existence of pathologies, and this shows us that human behavior cannot be completely governed by rationality.

Addiction depends on the character of the individuals involved; we're not all the same when faced with it.

Dependency is not a simple linear consequence of the product's power. Dependency takes root in favorable terrain. But my experience as a clinician has shown me that it's not easy to know which terrains are favorable. A strong correlation has been observed between smoking marijuana at the age of 18 and the beginning of schizophrenia . . . Nevertheless, marijuana doesn't produce schizophrenia all by itself; it does so in favorable terrain and in conjunction with a set of specific conditions. All this cannot be known in advance. At the heart of every practice, there's always this core of not-knowing.

Let's go back to these situated multi-resistances you're telling us about: will they suffice to change the order of things and reorient the world in a more desirable direction?

We can't know that. But at least these multiple experiences have one great quality, and that is that none of them claims to be the royal road to changing the world. These multi-situated conflictualities have shown the system's weaknesses. After the talk I mentioned earlier, a member of the audience reproached me for not naming capitalism as the main enemy. The problem is that by naming capitalism, we reestablish the old way of thinking that identifies a central point against which we must revolt. Although it's true that capitalism puts the living being in danger, its domination is exercised in a diffuse way and without any center. That is why capitalism as such cannot be attacked. Our target has to be, not big capital in the abstract, but the concrete processes through which it is manifested and against which it is possible to rise up and conquer.

But you don't envisage the possibility of a political change that would seek to improve society?

Political change is a hypothesis, a possibility, that could occur only in the event of a very extensive development of all these multi-situated actions, because only that will be able to produce other modes of production and relation regionally. The great historical error has been to think that we could pit global communism against global capitalism. The reason is that any globality is always captured by capitalism. The only real anti-capitalism is constituted by the myriad experiences I have mentioned. Of course, in the age of neoliberalism, capitalism is a horror whose excesses are acknowledged by even its theoreticians and most fervent supporters. From the IMF to Davos, everyone is now openly worried about the disaster that threatens us. In passing, we note the absolute impotence of these masters of the world to change the course of events. We may well grant that they aren't seeking ecological destruction, but because they are, paradoxically, held prisoner by their power, they can do nothing to avoid it.

But in our post-political world, the traditional parties are almost nonexistent, and labor unions are moribund . . . And the multi-situated actions you're talking about are precisely not politics in the traditional sense of the term.

Let's not forget that the politics practiced at the end of the nineteenth century and in the twentieth century had nothing in common with what Moderns identified as politics. For me, politics is a system that is linked to a specific period and is currently collapsing. Consider the idea of representation: it is to politics what the thermometer is to fever. Representation is not a problem in itself; it always follows when the objective context changes. But today, states engage in management, not politics. Politics is what takes place at the level of the people, of the power of the base, which exists in multiple ways. As for the representation of power, it's powerless, and it's concerned with management. Now, although we need more or less centralized management authorities in a complex world, the latter cannot be the site of either politics or power. And today, it's impossible to imagine what the most democratic forms of management might be. A greater power of resistance and alternative proposals would already have to exist before the question of changing institutions and representation could really be raised.

Such a change will not necessarily take place in two distinct phases. We can imagine lines of counter-power existing among elected officials. In Argentina, for instance, when we developed a critique of the government, two senators and a representative supported our wishes for a counter-power. We can therefore imagine officials supporting counter-powers, but for that to happen it's essential to turn the situation around: power must be preserved at the level of the base, not at the level of representation. Elected officials must be simple instruments of the movement. Obviously, that's difficult to bring about . . . At the end of the armed conflict, in the province of Buenos Aires, we had developed so many counter-power activities that we drew up an electoral list including friends and neighbors. But on the day after that list was elected, the representatives dissociated themselves from the base in order to establish their own power!

We began our discussion with the relationship between the digital world and the political and social transformations of our time, with one question in view: how is it possible, in this context both so novel and so difficult to understand, to take an emancipatory action that can deal with the challenges of protecting the living being and culture? By way of conclusion, what can you tell us?

We are passing through a dark period: traditional fascism is going hand in hand with returns to theocratic totalitarianism, along with the disciplinary management of the living being by means of AI, which devitalizes citizens. The destruction of the ecosystem and the threats endangering the possible ways of life on our planet are very real. Henceforth, although any search for an overall, simple solution is psychologically comprehensible, it is, paradoxically, part of the problem. While we're experiencing the moment that Foucault called the end of the era of Man, the question now is how to think and act in complexity, which comes down to asking on whom or on what we can act. Today, being on the left, being libertarian, entails coming to terms with this question. But above all, answering this question involves the urgent need to develop myriad forms of action without expecting results from them. The horizon has a genuine, inextricable dark core. And yet this will not inevitably lead to disaster, as long as we become capable of living in a multidimensional present, freed from the immediate and from promises. In short, today our times call upon us to think not about how to survive, but rather how to live in immanence, the sole site of transcendence.

ABOUT THE AUTHOR

Miguel Benasayag is a philosopher, psychoanalyst, and epistemology researcher. Born in Buenos Aires in 1953, he joined the resistance against the military junta and was arrested and imprisoned for four years. After his release he moved to France, where he became a researcher, clinician, and activist in the "new radicalism." He is an author and columnist.